MW00526411

American Parable

Sonia Greenfield

American Parable

poems by Sonia Greenfield

Coal Hill Review
Pittsburgh, Pennsylvania

Copyright © 2018 by Sonia Greenfield

All rights reserved. No part of this book may be reproduced in any form whatsoever without written permission from the copyright holders, except in the case of brief quotations in critical reviews or essays. For information contact: *Coal Hill Review*, 5530 Penn Avenue, Pittsburgh, PA 15206.

Author Photo: Alexis Rhone Fancher
Original Cover Photo: Yigithan Bal
Cover and text design: Kinsley Stocum
Titles and text set in Cheltenham

Printed on acid-free paper.

Coal Hill Review is an imprint of Autumn House Press, a nonprofit corporation with the mission of publishing and promoting poetry and other fine literature.

pennsylvania
COUNCIL ON THE ARTS

Autumn House Press receives state arts funding support through a grant from the Pennsylvania Council on the Arts, a state agency funded by the Commonwealth of Pennsylvania, and the National Endowment for the Arts, a federal agency.

ISBN: 978-1-938769-34-4

Table of Contents

There wasn't even any rioting in the streets.
People stayed home at night, watching television, looking for some direction.
There wasn't even an enemy you could put your finger on.

—Margaret Atwood, *The Handmaid's Tale*

Women & Children First

When the wind changes direction,
smoke shifts from the fires, so sometimes
it's burning tires in my face, other times
it's meat. Reader, I have done what I can
for you. Gave you my extra Sig
& taught you how to shoot, showed you
which mushrooms are safe to eat, even
trained you to avoid congregations
of carrion flies & the decay they make
love to. If food was plentiful, I shared it.
If the moon only shone on empty woods
or handfuls of bright sequins drummed up
by breeze across the lake, we laughed at
nothing in particular. Now, there's a menace,
a madman pulling off each fence board
at the rear of the yard & I'm crouching
with you, a few bullets left between us.
Reader, I have this child clinging to my leg,
his eyes crazed with fear, his sweaty face
flecked with dirt. The sounds of splintering
wood & hound-like baying make our hackles
rise. You look to me for help, but my field
of vision narrows, only able to take in
the one I would kill to save. I love you,
but you know how it has to be. Grab your
gun, Reader. Run, Reader. Lakshmi Singh
says the hordes are on the move &
from this point on you're dead to me.

Family Road Trip

You're pretty sure it's sagebrush
green blasted & bleached

by the sun. It always reaches
the horizon no matter where

the car points, clouds cast
shadows shaped like tortoises

that crawl across the desert.
Something subtle switches

as you cross: Joshua trees gather
then a sea of cacti no higher

than our knees. Husband
at the wheel, son singing

in the backseat & you
fiddling with the car's climate

press blue down for cool, red
up for hot. What you would die for

is already with you in a wagon
almost paid off. To ask

who you would die for will
never come to pass. The light

is long this time of year when
the border collects migrants who

had to answer: they found
an empty water bottle & photos

of children in the man's pocket
but had no idea who to call.

Museum of Love

Things were different
before The War, I guess.
An exhibit had photos
of something called *kissing*
& the interactive center
let you experience what they
called an *embrace*. I tried it
with a docent who smelled
of shampoo, though I did not
understand which way to turn
my head. It must have been
hard work back then. I admit
I got a little sad in the gallery
of drawings done by children
for their mothers. Those
crudely scrawled hearts
in shades of pink & scarlet
made my eyes water. One
room held books filled
with *love poems*, with lines
like *love is the shadow self*
of fear / though infused with light
its paradox the ache / that makes
us hold the word 'heart' / in our
mouths sometimes / afraid to swallow.
I didn't get it since so much
poetry, a dead art anyway,
depended on historical context.
When I left, they were debuting
the marriage wing & I heard
a peal of bells so sweet they
made my teeth ache, a sound
that hung in my ears
for hours afterwards.

From Nigeria to New Zealand

So men with Kalashnikovs,
red eyes & hand-rolled
cigarettes strap bombs under

the veils of girls as young as eight,
send them into the center of town.
Detonate. But those girls, their

girl faces, girl knees & girl
dreams wasted are not mine
to plug into a poem about disgust

here on the coast of California
where I lick & lick & lick the paws
of my sadness like a nervous habit.

Instead, consider the octopus
who escaped the ugly nubs
of human noses pressed to his tank

& the pits of their pink mouths
against his glass. He's mine.
Under ink cloak of night, lid off,

slime coat pulled close over all
eight flowing shoulders, down
the drain he split. *Fuck*

this noise, he said, to canned
clams & human cruelties
before suckering out to sea.

refugee

dear melania you can rest
awhile we know you rode
hard across the wasteland
to climb over this wall &
melania let us water your
horse let us send for your
only son hush now melania
no more tears put your head
in my lap & i'll untangle
those brambles from your
hair just think no more
injections melania no more
blue pills & morning catches
in our forest like a struck
match while night falls exactly
unlike a rolling up of tinted
windows more like the way
slovenian woods pull their
shutters closed at the end
of the day melania you must
be hungry like a mail-order
bride so we insist you eat
this bread then wash in
the brook you can sleep on
your escape because you will
have to get used to such a lack
of hands in you melania
your bed is over there

American Parable

Once, there was a country
where people were afraid.
They had weapons & open
spaces, prairie grass & forests,
river runs & rolling golden
mountains. It is said the people
kissed the faces of their children,
raised their flags, loved their dogs.
Word spread that terrible creatures
were shambling towards them
ready to destroy their factories
& spawn more creatures
to take over their land, beasts
that would give away their food
& firewood leaving them with
nothing but rusting tractors
& the endless cycle of news
flickering from enormous
screens. *Be afraid*, the faces said,
so they were, until a prophet
who lived in a golden tower said,
I will save you & the people
fell at his feet, though he never really
left his golden tower. *Throw your
rocks at those people*, he said,
they are to blame, so stones
flew at people who shared their land,
who kissed the faces of their children,
who raised their flags, who loved
their dogs, but who were different.
The prophet erected a wall & all
the worshipers huddled on one side.

They were not wrong about a golem
slavering towards them, though it was
amorphous, like a fog of plagues
& it could easily scale any wall.
The others left on the far side
heard the knell of a bell they already
knew, lit their torches & plunged
into the darkness, familiar as they were
with the art of survival. It was time
to get to work.

Harkening Back

We're at a dinner party
with real grown-ups &
the hosts say how much
they love their avocado lady
at the Farmer's Market
because she can sell you
the perfect avocado for today
& one good for Tuesday.
I say to my husband this
is what white people talk about
over cheese & olives, unoaked
chardonnay washing down
all that privilege. Naturally,
the conversation shifts &
the radiologist remembers
when his valley hospital was
one of the few with a unit
for what they used to call "Gay
Related Immune Deficiency"
& *all those mothers*, he says,
*would bring in their sons who
were so young*, he says & *dying*,
he says. Then like a bell
unrung, I am transported
back to my San Francisco
where these men I knew—
the last of the first wave,
before AZT & cocktails—
would succumb, like my
downstairs neighbor, charming
& volatile, how we would hear
fights with his boyfriend

after too many hours awake
hanging with crystal. Then
he was gone in a weekend.
Any time I would party
at a birthday for an old queen,
it meant something. It meant
another year. Lo! then science
happened & wards cleared out,
which is to say that distrust
of progress sickens me, that some
stupid harkening, a misguided
nostalgia for a retrograde past
would kill the men I love
who love men, so I don't want
your golly-gee & I would be
happy to wish you all back
into your cornfields & I wish
those mothers could just
have their boys back.

Ghost Ship

I have been that young, that electrified
by the bohemian scene of a city spilling its lights
all around me. I have been to parties
in sketchy spaces where painters have work
on the walls that should be seen by millions
but is seen by the few of us figuring out
who we're going to fuck after too much cheap wine
drunk from plastic tumblers & figuring out
how we're going to make it a country's width away
from families, struck out on our own
like explorers getting comfortable with being alone
in a wilderness that is actually just a room
rented in a house of strangers. I have been
that woman high on E, my eyes doll-dark, jaw
clenched, body ready to swallow pleasure
in a million lusty gulps. I know any space we inhabit
can become a ghost ship. I have read enough
to know stories of wildfires, of boats found
empty, of the soul yanked whole-cloth from
its innocent wearer. But you can't live in fear
of the apparition, the adventurers afloat on
their rickety structure & cast to a sea
of flames. It can happen at any time to anyone,
so when music flares up & takes hold of you,
when a swirl of colored spotlights sets you
spinning, you have to dance as if
the very act of living depends on it.

Yours

Suppose he was yours who saw rust
at first turn of the green wheel handle,
        your yard slicked down, sprinklers
ticking away days meted out in trips
        to 7-Eleven & the community pool.
Suppose he was yours who saw brown,
        waited for it to run clear, then drank
down the whole metallic feel of it
        from the copper end of a hose, summer
spread before him like a growing puddle.
        Suppose he was yours who bathed
in the river of your tub, scratched until
        his skin oxidized, flaking off in his sheets.
Suppose you saw pinpricks of his blood
        but washed those sheets in the same water
anyway. Suppose they said *boil it*
        & you did, but that only made it worse.
Suppose he was yours who was told
        his anger will fleck & spread unchecked,
was told bits of heavy metal will dam
        his lobes. Suppose he was yours who
was tested & told he will lose himself
        in a wash so sick everyone already knew
you couldn't eat the fish caught there.
        Suppose he said *I'm just going to be stupid*
anyway. What would well up in you
        & where would that poison run to?

Upon Misreading "Downed Statue of Robert E. Lee" as "Drowned Statue of Robert E. Lee"

Like deCaires Taylor's sunken sculptures
gathering coral in their crenulated lips, marble

wearing the green velveteen of algae, yellow
tangs schooling around their bowed heads,

a few filtered rays of sun rippling across
their still forms, send him & his horse down

into the silt-cloud off the Atlantic. Collect
Stonewall, Old Joe & General Morgan.

Gather the monuments & dump them
off a pier. Subsume them in the preserving salt

of our dark waters so if you want to touch
this history bad enough, you can dive for it.

Anyway, historians note that sharks learned
to follow ships along the slave route because

they fed on the bodies thrown overboard.
Where are the many glorious statues erected

to the men & women tossed there? Carve
them from African wood & prop them

on shore to let our American sun warm
what used to be flesh, the heart of a tree.

At least, then, I could reach out a hand
& touch what my forefathers wrought.

Museum of Extinct Peoples

I heard great things
about the Caucasian wing
from a descendant, so I had
to go. An interactive exhibit
let me handle objects like
scrunchies, which were used
to bundle hair, or the *lacrosse stick*,
which was a net at the end
of a long pole used in games
where pale men tried to prove
their mettle. I got to try
something called *scrapbooking*
& I learned whole stores
were dedicated to this art
primarily practiced by female elders
who created false documents meant
to obscure their children's failings.
One diorama held a wax family
in stasis at the dinner table:
a small, well-dressed nuclear unit
eating food cooked in a *wok*,
tools called *chopsticks* pinching
at noodles on their plates.
The plaque beside the exhibit
told how these tools didn't originate
with white people, but they used them
to appear tolerant of other cultures,
this ruse so deep they forgot to stop
once behind the locked doors
of their tidy houses. As I was
getting ready to leave I realized
that curators had scented the air
near the exit with fear. I could
hear it wheeze through the ducting,
the hair on my arms
lifting up as if to listen.

A Singular Penance

As if the act wasn't enough—the taking
children out of school to see it, the posses

built of the dispossessed, the jeering,
the rope, the guns, the flies, the fomenting

heat of a sickly summer—postcards were
made & sold, as if cruelty was worth

commemorating, yours to keep for a nickel.
At the center is the ancient oak coerced

into something it must want no part of,
the weight of its burden heavy where it

hangs from a lowermost limb as men
pose next to what their ruined hands

did, each wearing their best straw hats.
After walking the horses away & cleanup—

a son cut from the limb & buried, an image
branded on the eyes of his mother—the tree

persists as trees do when they are allowed to
& that region's history becomes sealed

in a capsule: The tree's ring of a year's
events, neither close to the scarred bark nor

fresh with new growth buried deep. Just there
in the middling quiet, too easily forgotten.

Snapshots of Pluto from New Horizons

The images come back
& our minds make a heart

of the variegated terrain,
the shape proffered with light,

as if we always default
to optimism even when we

append *dwarf* & take away
citizenship. Pluto teaches us

a lesson about modifiers,
how they sometimes count

us out. Add *autistic* to boy
& he spins around his class,

orbiting but never part of
the system. *Migrant* to worker

means existence on the edges
of our landscape, *anything*

to woman means eclipsed by
gaseous giants. On the outside

we submit our love letters
anyway, only wanting to be

adored. You get the picture:
NASA makes the most

of contrast so Charon squats
in the shadows & Pluto's

big heart leaks like
a torn sandbag.

Ringling Bros. and Barnum & Bailey

I am not afraid of clowns, but I
am afraid of clowns visiting pediatric
oncology, afraid of suspenders
& oversized shoes, greasepaint,

hooped pants, curly wigs & polka-dotted
ties showing up every week offering
balloon animals as if some quick diversion
could make everything OK. It's called

clown care, they go to clown college,
they're called clown doctors & it doesn't
make everything OK. But if we can smile
for a tender minute at the absurdity

of a squirting flower magicked from
a handful of handkerchiefs, a flower
pulled from a satin sleeve & proffered
to a girl with no hair, it must offer some

solace, or why else would Robin Williams
make a movie about it? I am not afraid
of clowns because my grandfather hung
a paint-by-number of Emmett Kelly's

Weary Willie & his Depression-era
grimace on the wall meant I was just five
& Robin Williams was still alive. My
grandfather too & my husband's Uncle

Harold, a clown doctor who dry-cleaned
his funny suit & showed up at Shriners
Hospital in St. Louis with his red rubber
nose in place & when a family flies in

for the best facility, leaving the family dog
with a neighbor, carefully packing suitcases
in the half-dark of desperation, drawing
the blinds on their house to seek their child's

last option, Ronald McDonald, that buffoon
who sells hamburgers, houses them, so I am
not afraid of clowns. I am not afraid of clowns
because Sondheim wrote "Send In the Clowns"

& Judy Collins sang it & who doesn't love
Sondheim & how could anyone begrudge
Judy Collins anything? We live in a post-clown
world where twisted men dress as clowns

to terrorize children, so it's no surprise
the circus is closing shop & rolling up
its big top. You can't send in the clowns
anymore if we don't know what they're for.

Alternate Facts

We never thought it could happen here—
the poisoned, the disappeared—

these tunnels a network of news channels—
server room, keyboards, screens aglow

on damp, earthen walls—the reporter
bludgeoned in her bed & found

by her daughter—see this passage here?
this is where we shuttle journalists

through to California—our cell towers
are disguised as olive trees, but drones

pick them off, so we rebuild—don't mind
these spiders: their venom is better

than state-sanctioned firing squads—
how we lost half our staff, their families—

& don't mind the darkness pressing
against you here in the underground—

it is the medium we move news through
now that the mobs have bought The Machine—

if I'm not back by morning, I was caught
& tortured by order of decree—

our Great Leader wants us all dead—
you, your loved ones & me.

No More

There weren't many shamans
left to carry on the antique practice,
so they had to teach us. How to sterilize
them, how to use them
as instruments, but then they
began to disappear—some effort
by The Machine to dismantle our network—
a halting production of wire hangers.
& cloth-covered ones wouldn't work
& molded plastic ones wouldn't work.
We did not use back alleys as they said,
but spot-lit living rooms with
plastic-covered sofas draped
in sterilized linens, our hands covered
with contraband nitrile gloves. When supplies
& practitioners became scarce,
surplus stores along Main Street sold
newborns to any white women
clutching crosses & checkbooks.

The Miami Beach Museum of Water

I'm sure if we had poets, they'd be writing about the swallowing of Miami Beach by the sea. —Bruce Mowry

Volunteers say take a laminated map. Depending
on the moon's pull, you can canoe along canals
or go under. The canals run through former hotel
lobbies, walls striped with shifting water lines or past
second-floor condo windows where rats float
in the middle of foam mattresses, but you're limited
by what's seeable on the surface. I take a tank & mask
then descend with light & fins to minnow through
the old bikini shop where suits on hangers are thick
with algae & mob-faced groupers make change
at the register. You can slip past a graveyard
of drowned palm trees moping like the ghosts
of surfers. At the Cuban restaurant, abandoned
mid-marriage of beans & rice, salt-corroded iron
frying pans stick to their burners, but I spend time
in the parking lot rifling glove boxes like that Escalade
encrusted by small colonies of corral. Nothing much
there but registration, two lipsticks, a small revolver
& an empty tube of sunscreen.

Dear Kim Jong-un

Do you work out? Because I've seen a lot of flexing
going on in statehouses while the rest of us
are just trying to figure out what to feed our kids
when they want nothing but pizza, so we come up
with novel ways to pair bread & cheese as if
we're fooling ourselves into thinking it's not pizza.
Do you like cheese? My son likes string cheese best,
Manchego second & sharp cheddar at a distant third.
I would be happy to feel your biceps if it would mean
endless bomb-free days of incognito pizza. Do you think
your ego is more Maine Coon in that it's big & plush
or is it more Siamese in that it is almost slick to the touch
& likes to talk loudly in the middle of the night
while you're trying to sleep? If you want I will stroke
your ego until it purrs if you put away your pet
submarine. I saw that picture of you posing
with your warhead & I really like your fur hat
but was a little surprised to see that nuclear annihilation
could be wrapped in a package that looks like a prismatic ball
meant to turn & toss reflected red spotlights
all over a club floor. Do you like to disco? My son
likes to play freeze dance at summer camp to songs
by Lady Gaga. I know under your double-breasted
khaki coat a heart beats same as mine. Do you like
children? My son has a beauty mark next to his mouth
& eyelashes every lady says she wants to steal.
He is made of cameo-pink incandescence & clumsy
grace. I can feel his guileless heart hammer through
the thin wall of his chest, which can't be much different
than your daughter's delicate ribs wrapping around her motor
as a hand cups a flame to keep it from blowing out.

I Believe, in the End, the Dogs Will Save Us

Not the St. Bernard with its cask of brandy
digging us from an avalanche. Not the Rat Terrier
flushing vermin from infested walls & crawl spaces.
Not the bomb-sniffing shepherd who couldn't learn
how loyalty leaves behind soldiers weeping
in their barracks. Not the retrievers, herders,
guiding eyes, or hounds. Just the mutt rescued
from a shelter & lost in early summer in a town
where a yearly carnival makes money for the firehouse
& families gather at the lake every season to grill
& wave away mosquitoes & see if their kids can finally
swim out to the buoy & back. The kind of town
fractured by an election year, where for the first time
ever, a swastika was spray-painted on the synagogue,
where a girl went door-to-door with flyers soon
stuck to refrigerators with magnets shaped like Florida
until everyone was talking about the lost dog,
an odd mix of spaniel & scrap that chased squirrels
across yards, which may be why a search party gathered
at the diner & headed for the woods to the right of town
in the late morning, cicadas already trilling through
a thickening heat. After only an hour, they found him
half-dead, his foot caught in a trap left over from autumn.
He must have been there for days the way his mouth
drew flies, the way the metal teeth had worked through
to bone. Once freed, the girl carried him home
in a dirty towel & the diner put out a large jar
to raise money for the vet bill. Everyone came in
with a dollar or two, but they were unable to save
the leg. When he hopped along as mascot of the July 4th
parade, all the citizens gathered at the curb to cheer
as he passed dressed in a sequined vest made
to look like an American flag, the sun flashing
on him in red, white & blue.

Acknowledgments

Thankful acknowledgment is made to the editors of the following publications where versions of these poems first appeared:

"Women & Children First" has appeared in the *Los Angeles Review*

"Family Road Trip" has appeared in the *Pittsburgh Poetry Review*

"Museum of Love" and "The Miami Beach Museum of Water" have appeared in *South Florida Poetry Journal*

"From Nigeria to New Zealand," "Ghost Ship," and "Dear Kim Jong-un" have appeared online for *Rattle's* Poets Respond

"refugee," "American Parable," and "Snapshots of Pluto from New Horizons" have appeared in *Verse-Virtual*

"Harkening Back" has appeared in *Lullaby of Teeth: An Anthology of Southern California Poetry* by Moon Tide Press

"Yours" and "No More" have appeared in *The Pinch Journal*

"Upon Misreading 'Downed Statue of Robert E. Lee' as 'Drowned Statue of Robert E. Lee'" has appeared in *Virga Magazine*

"Museum of Extinct Peoples" has appeared in *Menacing Hedge*

"A Singular Penance" has appeared in the online anthology *Over the Moon: Birds, Beasts, and Trees,* published by *poemeleon*

"Ringling Bros. and Barnum & Bailey" has appeared in *Crab Creek Review*

"Alternate Facts" has appeared in *Anti-Heroin Chic*

The *Coal Hill Review* Chapbook Series

Winner of the 2017 Prize
American Parable
Sonia Greenfield

Winner of the 2016 Prize
Herald
Roberta P. Feins

Winner of the 2015 Prize
English Kills
Monica Wendel

Winner of the 2014 Prize
A Green River in Spring
Matthew Thorburn

Winner of the 2013 Prize
The Welter of Me and You
Peter Schireson

Co-winner of the 2012 Prize
Prayers of an American Wife
Victoria Kelly

Co-winner of the 2012 Prize
Rooms of the Living
Paul Martin

A Special Edition
Irish Coffee
Jay Carson

Winner of the 2011 Prize
Bathhouse Betty
Matt Terhune

A Special Edition
Crossing Laurel Run
Maxwell King

Winner of the 2010 Prize
Shelter
Gigi Marks

Winner of the 2009 Prize
Shake It and It Snows
Gailmarie Pahmeier

Winner of the 2009 Prize
The Ghetto Exorcist
James Tyner